The Kissing Party

The Kissing Party

Sarah Barber

The National Poetry Review Press

The National Poetry Review Press
(an imprint of DHP)
Post Office Box 2080, Aptos, California 95001-2080

Printed in the United States of America
Published in 2010 by The National Poetry Review Press

978-0-9821155-8-9

Cover art:
Runaway
2003 oil on board 58cm x 60cm
Gillian Warden
www.gillianwarden.com.au

for my parents
and for Don, who gave this book its title

Contents

The Golden School

the kissing party

The kissing party was ending.
Kids went home for supper.
Kids went home to twin beds.
It was sad—oh yes, we were sad

and for nothing but the body
of the girl next door pretending,
through two lit windows, sleep
on a grass-green quilted coverlet.

Deliberately lit, calculatedly
curled, the curve of her hip
went disappearing into the dark
landscape between the legs.

That's the place where the longed-for
dead walk about without us.
In the parks of our childhood
in an endless afternoon:

birds asleep on their branches,
the sun as hot as a mouth,
and even under the shady leaves
nobody loves us, or will, ever.

the mechanical heart

still from a porno

Here we are in our bodies,
here we are on the couch when the dvd
with the inimitable timing
of insensible things skips, pauses

so that a girl who is taking
and taking a penis into her mouth
makes us come to a parenthesis—here

we are in our bodies,
all flushing and conscious
that they knew this as love—

while oh yes the god in his power
is descending: terrible, careless,
his wings in the immaculate silence beating
like what I used to call the heart,

like that obscenity the heart.

a grotesque

I oil my hair in the bath. That gluts
with gold a something delicate,
and like a shell, and pink, that fingers,
slipped along the ridge of collarbone,
dimpling all the skin, might seek.
Imagine whatever you require.
The Greek, in his splendid physique,
will accede. He is trying to believe
in his body. The caryatid is threaded
through, cunt to chin, with strings
to raise her arms as if the body were
a burden (take it in—how heavy it is,
how strong). I oil my hair in the bath.
Each nipple cuts the water like a new tooth.
Ah, we are trying to seduce you;
these are not questions to be answered.

a note in my copy of *phaedrus*

What if Apollo can
in powder blue parade all day,
then, looking down on that boy whose buttocks

are so firm in their proud
frown, give in, give his horses rein
enough for their no-nonsense ass-kicking?

I say, give gods their due.
That cart is like love is like strength.
We circle, admiring, these notable

rogues. We mark their speed. There,
in a myth of charioteer and horse,
they mean one does not feel how quick he's been,

in deciding *to love*
the boyfriend means *to lead his soul*,
to forgo the muscle's slow luxury,

nor how quick he's let go
the prize of erotic madness —
O small prize, no more to be carried off! —

for psychagogia.
That's transport. That's a car. Cue X,

who entered in a '77

Grand Prix. That chariot
left me stranded by the highway.
Poor hitchhiker!, but he wouldn't be moved.

What if Apollo can't?
Then what a girl needs is a winch,
and the man in the big truck to work it.

self-portrait, as landscape

Don't be afraid to do more than gaze.
There's no glaze against your fingers.
Is hers then the clear sight that holds out
no horizon? Well, no. But don't gloss
the pathetic, sir. So the heart's a mirror
carried in the eye, so love can't keep
its quicksilvered lenses long enough
for you two to fall into the sky. So what?
The body's not a glassed-in picture.
Just step back from the middle distance.
Look away if you cannot touch her.

how to wear jewelry

Stop fiddling with your earrings.
I know you're afraid that precious stone
is slipping from its silver hook,
is falling chiming to the sidewalk
or down the sink's expectant mouth.
Let it go. Not even care would redeem
the misery spent for that diamond
chip or those oysters' exquisite pains.
Remember the Princess Parizade,
whose principal dish was a cucumber
stuffed with pearls? She knew how
to wear jewelry, went out like Babylon,
lately sacked—remember her veils?—
could tell how a girl had lived
by her jewelry box: one crushed bead
of onyx—how did you ever manage
it?—a pendant of glass flowers, Italian,
snapped at the stem; one basket-weave
bracelet, grown too slim for the wrist;
gift after damaged gift. She knew
that a man can't live in the inside
of a pearl, knew that, if a girl's heart
will be hung on a fine silver chain,
anyday someone is going to break it.

cupid leaving the bed of psyche

Under her body he's caught his wing.
That's how you know it's morning
and time the god of love made his exit.
He rolls her over grinning, as he'll do
again forever, since the rising action
of the sun is just one more dart
in his erotic arsenal, a plaything
for tracing the bones of her shoulder
or tangling tomorrow into her hair.
Ah, was the night so short, again?
Have we come to the dangerous time
when somebody is waking a little
too quietly while the other sleeps?
In the myth, wax falls from a candle.
If they're both awake now it's time
you made the classical gesture. Leave.

(after Jacques Louis David's Cupid and Psyche)

a classical education can't save you from the radio

I looked up sky. I blued, obscured.
You were nowhere in my dictionary.

And the birds gave up reciting
their foreign vocabularies.
The clouds broke off their pas de deux.

Do do. The world is full of spit.
The sun's just a French pop song.

Do do, you do, you don't, you did
decline the thunderstorm, the chorus
girl and all her words for weepy.

during the special effects

The trees were undecided. So was I.
But la lune was on the up-and-up—

it was evening, or it was about to be—
and nature, in a heap of atoms,

was static and fuss. I felt you out
while you felt me up. We kissed

amidst some special effects:
bird dropped out of their nests, stars

ashed and burnt in our laps. In the simple
math of storm and porch and two

by two all over town, green girls
went down on their broken hearts.

It was all there in the quivering air.
And it had, in fact, been raining.

the distance to the moon

I call your attention to a Blake etching
where a short ladder points at the moon
and the man in the caption is crying,
I want! I want! Too sober. Too sad.

No, I wasn't around when you planned
this celestial body's pathetic end—

so *Cosmicomics* opens up on a white
nakedness which is shuddering
at the touch of the characters climbing on,
so you'd have us begin before we began to want—

but look (I'd have said) if you make desire
the matter you've made a story for its moral

denouement. And the moon may be
a lit sphere we chafe our hands on,
but if it only brings on the climactic
melancholy, you haven't been paying attention.

to the moon

The bedroom's black and unromantic. I
lie stoned on rapture, lack, the bright fact

of the body beside mine falling away
in the spectacular accident of every night:

you go to sleep for awhile, you rise—
luminous insomniac, ultraglide in white—

and, like the metaphysic incidental we
call heart, you cold you dark and fast.

we fall out of love

                              and into the sky.
But to dwell with intricate, endless
precision on fibres and films of moss
and lichen was never the plan. If you
were a leaf, you could not think *how strange,*
a leaf. You'd hang out out there, in the actual
blue outside the window of the bedroom
where, though we've read deeply into it,
we are finding the body is not the soul
made visible. And you wouldn't care,
adrift in the air, if the ether material
was restive in your nerves or the universe.
Meanwhile, we are having to invent
new words to settle the sky, the sick quiver
in it at evening. Lake blue. Infinity pool.
Your eyes if your eyes were blue.
Palisade, moth-wing, waxed moon blue.
Alloy, cerulean, old azure blue. The color
of longing with, finally, just landscape
behind it, the pure abstract color
of the unquiet heart and its *why*
at the vastness inside what is not quite
the body every big black oncoming night.

late archaic

If the heart were a city this would be its first
and oldest wall, here where the clay was worked

with steps where prostitutes and citizens
freely met with the night's pedestrian

longing here where the custom was to kiss
beneath the pandered moon, beneath the knowing

stars that lit the long way down to the sea—
here exiles turn their backs, traditionally.

still-life, with bruise

girl in a painted dress

A bird flares feathers
through a sky: he's herald
for that lion whose roar
crowds out the seams
of—what? shawl, shroud,
the costuming Pain
makes his pratfalls in?
Within the simplest
descriptions of a girl
on whose back and breast
there live a bird
and an embroidered lion
is just a body breathing
out. How like a fable!,
that begs us see,
through its attendant
pleasure-speaking
beasts, the trees
who make of soft wind
slurring their softly
moral speech: below
the watercolor wash,
below the flattered
fabric, even I am not safe
from affect. In a body
turned museum

the fragile frisson
of a bird against a sky
is just the impression,
not the flame, of fire.

self-portrait, with poultry shears

Jointed with a coil
and bar, a nut and bolt, they expand
on a familiar marvel—
spring and catch—unfasten
fast heft that's made

for larger hands. Held
together by a latch itself held
a-pivot, stainless teeth
partnered to the sharp shaft
let the shears stay

closed. So, they assume
a shape not unlike a dagger's, curved
to a crest, handled fine in
hammered steel. *Cut*'s not far
from *ornament*.

world's finest model horses

Midway through his proud first step—
all lifted head, all irritable lifted tail—
the Arabian, his cut nostrils flared
for the scent of saddle-leather, sights
you in his fixed black eye. But where
is the glint of the bit, of the buckle
on the bridle? He can't think why
you don't mount him, intelligent
as he is in these precise and heavy
hooves. Even the ground rises up
to meet their step, is never unsteady
under glorious legs. Don't tell him
the muscle he thinks he's flexing
to kick out, quickened with desire,
is thickened with plaster and painted on
with darker shellac. Don't tell him
he can't fall because he can't run.

erotic novel from the abruzzi

She cannot even tell the heroine's name—
maybe she's unbound, uncorseted, all
ragazza, present perfect at the novelist's
discretion, or ours, so we can leave
as it's getting less erotic than a wife's
flannelled belly swollen after much birth
(four in five years) and the doctor's mercy
hysterectomy; maybe she is stripped
down to *type*: nun, virgin nun, weak
for peonies, those sex-resemblers,
touching lips to them, rolling onto her fingers
to twiddle a mock Magnificat, a handmaiden
sort—and there are pictures which don't
surprise, but whose hand drew them here?
Stepfather, father, or mother who, eighteen,
lovely as a type, left the Abruzzi to home here
boarding strangers, renting room in her bed?
And which one of the fathers was it
who bedded a tree to bear figs (even
in Illinois) for preserves, the late-ripening
flesh kept present, reserved for him
to spoon over toast muttering *delicious*
like a folk-tale peasant girl who could not fill
herself full enough with figs. Sweet enough
to his taste though she did not like them, sucked
too slowly and the fig pulled away, tongue

left a moment to her fingers, salty
as this book is not, its illustrations more dry
than any pornography she's seen where sex
looked damp, large-breasted, hard-nippled,
had long tapered legs that did not end
in ankles, the banal body excised by the frame:
a body like her own displayed, fucked
with looking. The nun in the novel enjoys
what is being done to her. She will not
get pregnant a fifth time, not even once,
with doctors more tender than merciful,
half up the ropeladder and promising
the peonies gentleness and absolutely
nothing lurid until they've had their fill.
Everywhere but a brief flowering.

the cardinal sees a dirty picture

Paint, you old pander, again
you miss your way to the heart.
Who's roused to heresy these days
is claimed by its subtler art.

But how does a devil enter there?
Like an arrow tapped through the chest.
And what does he within?
Cricket's work, black and tuneful,

his wings a carriage for despair.
And how do we force him out?
An organ that does not open must
be cleft as buttocks. Pincers in

and look, the testicle without its skin!
Make a man of two asses,
spank him behind and before.
Get thee on thy ways to sin no more.

gloss for a fable

In the story behaving itself, a fox
pursues a priest to water. No one falls in;
no one sinks. No one is thinking
of that oldest character in the fable,
the soul, which sits on the margins
anyway, taking notes in an italic hand.

still-life, with bruise

This fruit, of course, was rotting
while the painter painted. Do not mistake me;
these were not the strawberries daubed
with fantastic mold in the glass museum,
not even the rind, with its coat of wax
and fruitflies, of the cantaloupe I failed to eat
all week because my lover had not come.
He had those perfect curving brows
of the Caravaggio boys, the thick pink
lips, the heavy cream skin. Young and broke,
he occasionally sucked sweet-vinegar
juice from an overripe matron in exchange
for rent that winter in the warehouse
of the local art league. It was cold. The windows
cracked like loose bits of lace, and every day
the same knife sank into the same fat slab
of plastic-wrapped cheese. Then you would
have done it, too, coated your anus, rammed it
with the blunt point of the difficult sculpture
no one ever came to see—a pure aesthetic
response to that something cold in art
that does not care for us, as after our supper
of milk and peaches, he stood behind me
at the mirror, laced our fingers, traced the line
running down to the mons veneris, stopped.
Why put yourself at risk by becoming beautiful?

The Arab in the overcoat was not an angel;
when they found me naked in the field,
that much became clear. Picture it
and try not to think of a Renaissance still-life:
blue bruise on the bare plucked thigh.
A teenage girl is just another sort of game bird.
And as for this terrible gorgeous fruit,
the resin-hued grapes and pomegranate, sour-apples,
plums and peaches and pears, the blood-red gape
of the fig-throat, the melon quartered, splayed
open with rot—it is only the most expensive
form of riot the painters knew, the one the body
always already is yielding to. And the scent
in his studio was the same rich perfume
of decay that hung thick and sweet
in his lungs, in his heart, in his humid blood.

advice to a boy on a roof in november

You're a heavy cloud, dropped
slow and settling its white
slates low on a gray slate roof
where snow comes down so
like snow, in all a soft
dissolving foreground, false
to the hard and far below.
Try to keep hold of your soul.

the archbishop at court

Here evil made an appearance,
not its first: the pin-pricks
to the keyhole finding sin a door,
a mouth, a crack, lubricated,
easy to slip into, a state
of the body like the sleep
of the not incorruptible behind
their doors where they can be left
to sleep or not. Always, among
the well-adjusted, are some
who are not, of whom the mystery
of iniquity admits nothing
except look out, look out.

allons enfants

Add this to rhetoric: a rock.
The intellectual, fast descending from
the podium, jerks his elbow,
masturbates his politics.

Was it for that you gave up
sodomy, Byron? As, to spite the Austrians
who wore those pompous epaulettes,
Venice once quit smoking (add this:

torches and a military
march), for they'd given up applauding long before.
Elsewhere, surely, there's an exploding.
But fatherlands are dead to us.

the golden school

the plate of grapes

Nobody was getting any younger
sitting there at the table waiting
for a word to rise, more luminous
and real than morning or rain

coming down as it came down
outside, glass-globed and glinting
in the perfectly meaningless dark.
And then, after the lightning,

there they were, the gods—
explaining nothing. They couldn't
even speak. It was the first morning
in their bodies. It was a golden age.

And they stared at the world
which was not new, as if, for awhile,
day would be day and grapes
swell under a frankly sensual sun.

aubade

And after the loves, after the others
with their rough or gentle ineffective hands,
forget how you were dreaming then,
dreaming to the sick quick metronome
the heart kept beating, too hectic
from speed and cigarettes to sleep,
though someone hushed all night
as if to hold you dreaming that long,
dreaming the moon was a marble
put in your palm to finger and forget
how the fidget-birds at morning rise
inevitable, and no dreaming holds them off.

yesterday, the crane

caught me up after two day's want
of sleep. Well, wasn't that sweet
unconscious mechanical drop
once something like heaven? And God
so careful an engineer he gauged
the weight of restlessness—exactly
my body in its plummet to nothing—
against His pulley, soul? That cord
kept taut, and its hook was a naught
whose function was lift, let me go
after a crane and through a conceit
and back to the seventeenth century.
But I never believed. I mostly didn't
even read the works we undid,
line by line unfastening sense
from sensory (like touch, given us
as if just for its excellence—hand
on my hip! hand in my hand!)
while afternoon blew by glorious
blue and the usual hipsters outside
the engineering building waited
for who-knows-what which these days
looks to me like it won't ever come
to lift me—from desire—up.

to a ring i lost planting bulbs

You give me the slip between garlic and lilies,
as if this is what comes of my unprotected
loves, of my hands in the sweet earth,
their willful miscegenation of the border bed
where you're tucked in deep with tulips, too,
like just one more of their heart-freaks:
a fluke diamondine flake, a thin vein gone gold.
Being mine, you'll grow up a girdled tree, girt
with a ringed-around root, nothing like
the fruitful vine of good wives—one of which
I'll never be so, my not-love-knot, you may
as well come up instead like a kiss:
the one wind gives to rouse the Japanese maple,
October's aerialist, its bright aureole
in the last late sun a red mouth, opening.

a note to the air

An alley of trees
whose white lace
blooms

(like women)
gives me

headache.
Along the sewage
river's lead

fence, seed pods—
all milk-whiteness

in a rush
of wind. And sky,
so far above, don't

ever bend
to touch my nose.

late birds

If sometime after supper you walk
down to Douglas Park where all summer
the birds of the neighborhood gathered,
you will probably not be thinking
that this is the place where the birds
would be if it were not already winter.
But it is. And so here is your heart
in its sweatercoat, and here is your heart
in its moccasins waiting for birds already flown.
It was autumn, there was that great black beating
of wings that blows open the soul.
Could you have done things differently,
caught, once, their particular art
of rising and finally been exalted?
Of course not. Of course not.

a scene from the renaissance

Lemon balm, mint, elderflower.
Under his arbor, this prince
in his body of glass—weary of love
or pleasure or action—seems
like no fragile manufacture.

And if you want a garden, too,
you'll start with your idea
of color: green green green for spiderplant,
elephant's ear, Lenten rose.
Out under the common daylight

we could drop the mirror we hold
to Nature, replace the sun
with clusters of yellow cosmos, level
hills, clear the creek-bed, color
the sky with lavender-flowers,

and hold the whole world just as still as—
a statue under a trellis?
Right. Here's the cue for those youths on horseback—
with their level glances, proud
patient lips, chastened reins, their whole

bodies in exquisite service
nerved for the celestial,

for that spasm in the shining fretwork
of the animate—who lift
the mirror, and cannot fix it still.

(after Walter Pater)

there is a garden in her face

But the sonnet lady is a slut, my students say—
as if a girl, or bird, or vase should restrain
our longing, as if we'd want them to. They don't,
I think, believe in beauty. And though
the body can be polished to inanity—
there the flower's as frequent as the leaf—

the landscape can feel, and is glad of her too,
was all the poets meant. The world's so bare
already: this bird no more than a drift of air
in the form of plumes, this sky from science tubes,
and that girl loved out in the medicinal lace-
weed, the one the universe clung to, a cloud
hovering low—was cropped above the waist
and blonde. You sang her the one that goes brick, house.

self-portrait, in botanical garden

Like a jaundiced heart, in throbs of gold
and yellow, the koi thrash, pack
belly on back for a living dam of mouths.

On its concrete piles the footbridge
does not shudder; the water in the next pond
hardly makes a pockmark
in a surface of lilies whose pads, outspread,
propose to bear a body-weight.

Amorous reeds are played on by the wind.

One ought not touch any of it.

the lawn mower

When we finally flip it over
the fireflies are out. The neighbor boy
has had his stitches in so I can admit
I think it is all fantastic: the suck
of the spark plug undone, the stuck blade
bent into the guard, and the sound
of the hammer's head reshaping the metal.
In this our suburban Eden we've only
a teenage Adam too dreamy to manage
his motorized scythe and silly Eve leaving
her coffee cups and plastic plant pots
behind in the grass. Though it's a long way
from a fall, this spring's first disaster,
I did like the thin thread of red
on his upper lip, and I like my mower
turned over among the glow-worms,
a monstrous dandelion as unnatural as we
are, out in a garden, untidily
golden and dangerously sharp.

gerard hopkins, reflected in a lake

My own impulse would show sky
in lake. Let blue on blue efface
the eye which sees both blues.
You can see I don't believe
in immanence: the landscape
I look at looks back, reflective
of the lack I stress it with.
But then, my vision's bad.
Your own's so sharp you sketch
it shaded, two black lakes.
As if the pupils overcame
their eye-holes. Like a skull.
Whose memento mori do you see
when light dilates to dazzlement,
draws sight, at last, wide open?
Not the soul's. Your own has eyes
which could not be closed.

not singing

Small intelligences on the upper branches—
birch and very white—black
themselves, burning, on the eye like sparks
catching now that branch, now this,
so that I turn my head to the superimposition
of another tree on the empty sky.
My eyes are bad. The birds are mad atwitter.

the big bad wind

It comes in and fucks everything up:
suddenly the backyard empties out
its trees and the ground gets trashed
with beer-bottle brown and beer-bottle green.

Darling, it was a real good party
but it's time you got off my couch.
Every apocalypse is just a joke
apocalypse, a fierce black birdie

who flew at the front door's glass;
every ending disappoints.
All these leaves and these feathers —
might some god show up to collect them?

bird lawn

Though leaves collect their yellow tongues
to strop the thousand blades of sky
and make them cut out pain, someone
is forever coming up the garden
with a palette and a brush
demanding an exact location for the light
that dazzles. An aesthetics of injury
is easy enough. Grass nubs itself down to the quick.
Even the birds silence themselves, refusing,
with judicial vigor, the longing to rise.

the golden school

Yellow tones to mustard, goes gold
and then horizon-lines itself with white,
blues off into a distance he's hung
at the foot of his bed. I know

there's no landscape like this one,
not even in memory, not in mine. I try
and it's always the nineteenth century:
on the edge of Lake Como an ersatz

ex-pat on a faux palazzo patio with yes,
a mountain, the open air, cold
coffee in an enamel cup—and here's the soul
and its parse, its partition, its part

with the body, ascend as a bird
beyond the eye whose sentimental lens
sees nothing real. The young lady
is inevitably sketching, says James.

Gold, gold, goes the Rothko; gold,
and no evading metaphor, no local color.
I know. But I'd have a night, an evening,
an afternoon he told me as a series

of summers, sun down like nothing

I know of the sunset, sun down in a room
they broke into, abandoned, the 80s,
the college girls gone home, acid and sun

ever more acidic, orange and red
and flame-out against the glass
I could not have brought myself to break,
I who make longing a professional career.

more light

Such spectacle as sun makes, rising,
makes the eye that sees grotesque
the show: the world will take its turn,
in white, as abrasive powder dropped
(to what effect, the artificer
of the drama doesn't say) on stage.
If the boards laid edge to edge
weren't groaning like a body
that would break if it knew how
to best display violence for delight,
if light would wear a costume
other than the heart's, or move more softly,
a ghost in a fantastic snow —
but for what other audience
than this, that can drop the curtain
if it wish, shall I have sun put on
an awful conscious grace?

Notes

"A Grotesque" – threaded through, cunt to chin – Ian McEwan's *Atonement*

"Self-Portrait, with Landscape" – the clear sight of love holds out no horizon – John Ruskin

"How to Wear Jewelry" – a man cannot live in the inside of a pearl – Ruskin

"During the Special Effects" – nature in a heap of atoms – Dryden and Handel's "Ode for St. Cecilia's Day"

"We fall out of love" – to dwell with intricate and endless precision on fibres of moss and lichen – Ruskin

"Allons Enfants" – to spite the Austrians the Venetians quit smoking – John Julius, Norwich, *Venice: Paradise of Cities*

"The Plate of Grapes" – try to grow grapes by the luminosity of the word day – Paul de Man

"There is a Garden in Her Face" – the landscape feels and is glad of it also – Walter Pater

Acknowledgments

Georgetown Review: "Cupid Leaving the Bed of Psyche"

The Journal: "A Grotesque" and "Self-Portrait, with Poultry Shears"

Juked.com: "A Classical Education Can't Save You from the Radio"

Malahat: "Aubade"

Memorious: "Still-Life, with Bruise"

Mid-American Poetry Review: "The Plate of Grapes"

The National Poetry Review: "Still from a Porno"

Poetry: "The Mower" and "To a Ring I Lost Planting Bulbs"

Southern Poetry Review: "The Archbishop at Court"

Western Humanities Review: "Erotic Novel from the Abruzzi"

www.ingramcontent.com/pod-product-compliance
Lightning Source LLC
Chambersburg PA
CBHW022031090426
42739CB00006BA/373